The Silk Road

Overland Trade
and Cultural Interactions
in Eurasia

Essays on Global and Comparative History

A series edited by Michael Adas

Other titles in the series:

Essays on Global and Comparative History

The Silk Road:
Overland Trade and Cultural Interactions in Eurasia

by

Xinru Liu

With a Foreward by Michael Adas, Series Editor

American Historical Association
400 A Street, SE, Washington, DC 2003

XINRU LIU is a professor at the Institute of World History, Chinese Academy of Social Sciences, in Beijing. She is the author of *Ancient India and Ancient China: Trade and Religious Exchanges*, A.D. *1–600* (Oxford University Press), *A Social History of Ancient India* (Press of Chinese Social Sciences, Beijing), and *Silk and Religion: An Exploration of Material Life and the Thought of People*, A.D. *600–1200* (Oxford University Press).

AHA Editor: Amy Smith Bell

Published in 1998 by the American Historical Association. As publisher, the American Historical Association does not adopt official views on any field of history expressed in this book.

Library of Congress Cataloging-in-Publication Data

Liu, Hsin-ju.
   The Silk Road:overland trade and cultural interactions in Eurasia /
Xinru Liu
     p. c..m. – (Essays on global and comparative history)
   Includes bibliographical references (p.).
   ISBN: 087229-106-5 (pbk.)
   1. Silk Road.   2. Asia–Relations–Europe.   3. Europe–Relations–Asia.
   4. Asia–Commerce–Europe. 5. Europe–Commerce–Asia. I. Title. II. Series.
DS329.4.L59 1998
950'.2—DC21   98-22781
                                     CIP

Printed in the United States of America

Contents

Foreword

Given the previously rather peripheral position of global and comparative history in the discipline, the growth of interest in these fields over the past three decades or so has been truly remarkable. The appearance of numerous works by prominent scholars on transcultural interaction and on variations in social systems and political economies, the great proliferation at both the college and secondary-school level of courses on world history and numerous textbooks with which to teach them, and the formation in recent years of the World History Association, an affiliate of the American Historical Association, all testify to the increasing importance of global and comparative scholarship and teaching within the historical profession. In some ways these developments represent a revival, for world or cross-cultural history is as ancient as Herodotus, and it enjoyed particular favor among Western intellectuals from the eighteenth to the early twentieth centuries. But challenges to the grand designs or underlying "laws" that writers like Spengler or Toynbee discerned in human history, as well as an increasing emphasis on area specialization within the discipline as a whole, led to doubts about the feasibility or even the advisability of attempting to generalize across vast swaths of time and space. In scholarship, world history came to be seen as a pastime for dilettantes or popularists; in teaching, it was increasingly equated with unfocused social studies courses at the secondary-school level.

Though the current interest in global history reflects a continuing fascination with the broad patterns of human development across cultures that were the focus for earlier works on world history, the "new" global or world history differs in fundamental ways from its predecessors. Writers of the new global history are less concerned with comprehensiveness or with providing a total chronology of human events. Their works tend to be thematically focused on recurring processes like war and colonization or on cross-cultural patterns like the spread of disease, technology, and trading networks. Their works are often more consciously and systematically comparative than the studies of earlier world historians. Partly because the research of area specialists has provided today's scholars with a good deal more data than was available to earlier writers, the best recent works on global history also display a far greater sensitivity than the more comprehensive world surveys to cultural nuances and the intricacies of the internal histories of the societies they cover. In addition, few practitioners of the new global history see their task as one of establishing universal "laws" or of identifying an overall teleological meaning in human development. Their main concerns are the study of recurring processes and the dynamics and effects of cross-cultural interaction. Depending on their original area orientation, global and comparative historians adopt these approaches because they see them as the most effective way of bringing the experience of the "people without history" into the mainstream of teaching and scholarship, of relating the development of Europe to that of the rest of the world, or of challenging the misleading myth of exceptionalism that has dominated so much of the work on the history of the United States.

This series of essays is intended to provide an introduction to the new world history. Each pamphlet explores some of the interpretations and understandings that have resulted from cross-cultural and comparative historical studies undertaken in the past three or four decades. The pamphlets are designed to assist both college and secondary-school teachers who are engaged in teaching courses on world history or courses with a comparative format. Each essay is authored by an expert on the time period or process in question. Though brief lists of works that teachers might consult for more detailed information on the topic covered are included in each of the pamphlets, the essays are not intended to be bibliographic surveys. Their central aim is to provide teachers facing the formidable task of preparing courses that are global or cross-cultural in scope with a sense of some of the issues that have been of interest to scholars working in these areas in recent decades. The essays deal with specific findings and the debates these have often generated, as well as broad patterns that cross-cultural study has revealed and their implications for the history of specific societies. Although all of the essays are thematically oriented, some are organized around particular historical eras like the age of Islamic expansion or the decades of. industrialization, while others are focused on key topics like slavery or revolution. Because there are many approaches to global history, these essays vary in format and content, from ones that are argumentative and highly inter- pretive to others that concentrate on giving an overview of major patterns or processes in global development. Each essay, however, suggests some of the most effective ways of dealing with the topic or era covered, given the current state of our knowledge. In recognition of the quincentenary of Columbus's "discovery" of the Americas, the series begins with an essay on the impact of the processes set in motion by his voyages. Subsequent pamphlets cover topics and time periods from the era of early European overseas expansion to the present and then from the era of expansion back to the time of the Neolithic Revolution.

Michael Adas, Series Editor
Professor of History
Rutgers University

Acknowledgements

To accomplish this work, I owe a great deal to Professor Lynda Shaffer, who suggested that I should be the person to write on this topic for the American Historical Association's Essays on Global and Comparative History. I am also greatful for her valuable advice and suggestions and for her editorial instructions on every detail in this essay. However, whatever mistakes remain, they are mine.

1

The Silk Road

THE SILK ROAD IS A TERM OFTEN APPLIED TO THE TRANS-EURASIAN TRADE routes that flourished during the first millennium of the common era. For more than a thousand years many luxury goods, of which silk was the best known, moved along these routes—either all the way from East Asia to the Mediterranean and vice versa or on their various segments and branches. The Silk Road was not a single route, nor did it remain stable throughout its existence. Depending on variations in environmental, political, and social conditions, the many branches of the Silk Road rose and fell in their frequency of use. Despite these changes, however, the Silk Road was Eurasia's most significant carrier of goods and cultural influences before the eleventh century, when maritime routes expanded and eventually took over the lion's share of intercultural trade.

REDISCOVERY OF THE SILK ROAD

Because of the predominant role of maritime trade routes in late medieval and modern times, the Silk Road fell into oblivion for many centuries. In addition, Mongol conquest and the later Mongol empire, though short lived, changed the infrastructure and mechanisms of transaction throughout Eurasia, and the once-flourishing ancient routes were almost forgotten. Only in the late nineteenth century did a handful of scholars-cum-adventurers begin to reveal art treasures and architectural remains buried in the settlement ruins along the most crucial segments of the Silk Road—those around the Taklamakan Desert in Chinese Central Asia. These ventures took place during a period when China was weak politically, and its government could neither protect the treasures nor prevent them from being taken to other countries.[1] The extremely dry climate, coupled with extremes of heat and cold, made this desert one of the most inhospitable lands on earth. But it also preserved many artifacts that are evidence of the interactions of many peoples, as well as evidence that testifies to the material and cultural prosperity of Chinese Central Asia for more than a thousand years.

Near Khotan, in western China, in the bitter winter of 1895, the Swedish explorer Sven Hedin found the ruins of an oasis settlement he called "Taklamakan," later identified as Dandanuilik. In 1899 he discovered Loulan, a Chinese garrison town of the Han dynasty. Following in Hedin's steps, the Hungarian Aurel Stein, a member of the British knighthood, started a series of excavations at Dandanuilik, which resulted in his sending of numerous antiquaries to the British Museum. Stein's explorations eventually led to the discovery and removal of the hidden library at Dunhuang. Though Hedin found the ancient sites, he was more of a geographer than an archaeologist. Stein led more excavations and thus made more contributions to discovering the deserted sites along the Silk Road.[2] After these initial excavations, Germans, Japanese, French, and finally Americans arrived in Chinese Central Asia, seeking the Silk Road's treasures. Before Chinese authorities finally closed the door to foreign adventurers in the early 1930s, because of pressure from the Chinese intelligentsia and the growing awareness of the general public, "the vast quantity of antiquities which they [foreign excavators] removed were to end up in more than thirty museums and institutions spread across Europe, America, Russia, and the Far East."[3]

Although these foreign adventurers and archaeologists underwent great physical hardship (some even risked their lives to recover manuscripts, murals, and artifacts from Chinese Central Asia) and were considered heroes in their own countries, Chinese intellectuals and many commoners considered them robbers of the Chinese cultural tradition. In any case, this distribution of cultural remains caused an interest in, or at least a curiosity about, the ancient Silk Road. In recent decades expeditions sponsored by the United Nations and various governmental institutions have traveled through the Central Asian deserts, enjoying much more modern facilities and transportation than those earlier explorers who surveyed and studied the ancient urban sites. Despite historical resentment about the loss of these cultural treasures, Chinese scholars have actively sponsored and participated in such research and conferences.

In addition to focusing on archaeological and art historical topics, research on the Silk Road has also concentrated on the tedious but extremely important work of deciphering ancient scripts and reading the extant manuscripts. From the late nineteenth century to the early twentieth century, several scholars-cum-explorers published their findings of art works from Central Asia. German scholars Albert Grunwedel and Albert von Le Coq are two such examples. Of the extant manuscripts and inscriptions, philologists and epigraphists deciphered several ancient Indo-European languages, including Sogdian, Khotanese, and Tucharian—W. B. Henning on Sogdian; A. F. Rudolph Hoernle, Sten Konow, and Ernst Leumann on Khotanese; and Emil Sieg, Wilhelm Siegling, and Werner Thomas on Tucharian were vanguards in deciphering these lost languages, although some of their works are only of historical value now.[4] The efforts to edit and translate documents in relatively known scripts and languages were no less strenuous. The English translation of Kharoshthi[5] documents in various Prakrit languages (northern Indian ancient vernacular languages) by Thomas Burrow is still of value.[6]

The cave library of Dunhuang held a large collection of written materials, primarily in vernacular Chinese. Chinese scholars made every effort to catalog and edit these materials, despite the fact that they were spread all over the world. In 1957 Wang Zhongmin compiled *Dunhuang Guji Xulu*, one of the early Chinese catalogs of Dunhuang documents.[7] An English catalog, compiled by Lionel Giles, was published in the same year, but it includes only those manuscripts that are housed in the British Museum.[8] Today most of the Dunhuang documents have been published as photoprints by various publishers. Many Chinese scholars are devoted to studying those precious historical materials. Among scholars who write in English, Victor Mair probably would have made more achievements than others, reading and editing these documents that are written in familiar-looking scripts but are full of pitfalls (most authors of these papers did not belong to the literate elite of their times).[9]

The mystery behind those scripts and the number of beautiful artifacts, including many pieces of silk textiles, invokes images of the luxurious life led by ancient and medieval peoples. These images were particularly striking against the bleak landscape of the Central Asian desert. With the accumulation of artifacts in museums and manuscript information in libraries, one starts to ponder the more fundamental and broader questions: Where did the wealth that supported these art works come from? If this flourishing urban culture of the desert depended on the Eurasian long-distance trade of luxury goods, what desires motivated the trade, and what were its transaction mechanisms? To explore these questions further, a brief survey of the rise of the Silk Road follows.

WEST AND EAST STARTED TO REACH EACH OTHER

Alexander's invasion of India in the late fourth century B.C.E., although a hot topic in Western historiography, only caused a few political ripples in India, which died out very quickly.[10] Cultural consequences persisted for centuries, however. After the invasion the Hellenistic world started to become acquainted with India and other Asian countries. Many exotic Indian goods and customs were reported to the Greek world, including cotton that grew on trees and seric fabric (silk) that was made from tree bark.[11] The Greeks bequeathed their knowledge of silk (that it came from a kind of tree) to the Romans, who accepted this without question for many centuries, even during the period when they demanded and acquired silk from the East in large quantity. After Alexander's invasion the Hellenistic world, especially the Seleucid neighbors of India's Mauryan Empire, had frequent friendly exchanges with India, despite some initial conflicts. Mauryan rulers sent exotic oriental products as gifts to the Seleucids, including 500 elephants, some ivory, and cotton textiles. Elephants captured the imagination of Westerners and became a topic of art, although they never became a commodity in high demand. But silk, only vaguely known to Greeks at that time, did. As the only silk supplier of that time, Han China was interested in exchanges with the West, but not because they wanted to sell their silks. Rather, the Chinese ruling elite were more interested in acquiring exotic items from the West.

Soon after the Han dynasty (202 B.C.E.–220 C.E.) reunified a war-torn China at the end of the third century B.C.E., the empire had to deal with frequent intrusions from the Xiongnu, a nomadic federation from the steppe. Although the rise and expansion of the Xiongnu had encompassed many nomadic groups, they had also driven others, such as the Yuezhi, westward. To deal with Xiongnu threats, the ambitious Han emperor Wudi (ruled 141–87 B.C.E.) sent an envoy, Zhang Qian, to seek an east-west alliance with the Yuezhi in 139 B.C.E. It took thirteen years for Zhang Qian to reach Bactria (in modern Afghanistan), where the Yuezhi had settled, and return to the Han capital, Changan. He was twice imprisoned by the Xiongnu, for a total of eleven years. Despite his efforts, Zhang Qian did not convince the Yuezhi to fight the Xiongnu.

Zhang Qian did bring back a knowledge of these "Western Regions" to the Han court, however. While continuing to send military expeditions to fight the Xiongnu, Wudi also dispatched various trade envoys to obtain exotic foreign goods from the Western Regions. One of these envoys, whom Wudi had sent to Ferghana to purchase a famous species of "blood-sweat" horses, was killed by the local ruler, an ally of the Xiongnu. Angered by the provocation of the Ferghana king and by the obstacles to obtaining the "heavenly horses," Wudi sent punitive expeditions under the command of General Li Guangli to Ferghana in 104 and 102 B.C.E. After the failure of the first expedition, General Li Guangli finally conquered Ferghana and collected its best horses for the Han Empire. Thereafter, horses from the Western Regions became one of the most important status symbols in China, no less important than imported cars are in China today.

Han emperors, like many rulers in the ancient world, soon realized that the cost of obtaining rare goods from far away through military expeditions was too high.[12] The horses of Ferghana were paid for by both many soldiers' lives and a large sum from the state treasury. Commercial exchanges would provide a better means. To open a trade route to the west, the Han government extended the Great Wall westward and built the Jade Gate to the west of Dunhuang. In addition to sending periodic expeditions, the Han government established garrison stations in its northwest frontier region. To guarantee trade traffic through the Tarim basin, the government also made alliances with the oasis states along the edge of the Taklamakan Desert. Soon exotic goods from Central Asia and further west appeared at the Han court and in the homes of elites: horses, furs, and woolen carpets from Central Asia; cotton textiles, pearls, and crystal from India; coral from the Mediterranean; glassware from the Roman world or from India; and various fragrances and spices from India, the Arabian Peninsula, and East Africa.

By the time the Romans held hegemony in the Mediterranean world, silk had become one of the most demanded Asian goods, because of Roman trading ties with India.[13] Trade between the Roman world and South Asia started long before the Christian era through Arabs. Arabian traders supplied Romans with spices and fragrances, either products of the Arabian Peninsula or from further east. Romans once believed that the Arabian Peninsula was the end of the "Spice Route." After envoys from various Indian states visited the Roman emperor Augustus (27 B.C.E.–15 C.E.), however, contacts with India became frequent. In the first century C.E. the Greek merchant Hippalus was said to have discovered, or learned from Arabs, how to ride the trade monsoons on the Arabian Sea. Roman ships (more specifically, Egyptian-Greek ships) left the Red Sea and followed the trade monsoons on the Arabian Sea to reach Indian and African ports.

A manual of navigation, *Peripulus Maris Erythraei* (The Periplus of the Erythraean Sea), recorded the ports and markets visited by Roman traders as well as the items they traded.[14] The most important ports on India's western coast were Barbaricum at the mouth of the Indus River and Barygaza on the Gulf of Cambay, an inlet of the Arabian Sea. Roman traders brought gold and silver coins, silverware, coral, wine, sweet clover, and perfume from Italy and other Mediterranean countries; glass, clothing, and styrax from Egypt and other eastern provinces; more wine, chrysolith (or topaz), dates, antimony, red orpiment, and frankincense from the Persian Gulf and the Red Sea; and slaves and colorful girdles of unknown origin.[15] From the Indian ports of Barbaricum and Barygaza, Roman traders returned with goods indigenous to various parts of India: indigo, ivory, cotton cloth, onyx stones, and long pepper.[16] They were also interested in bdellium, textiles, lycium, and spikenard from the Himalayas, costus (a spice) from Kashmir, turquoise from the mountain range known as the Hindu Kush, and lapis lazuli from Badakhshan.[17] Some other goods were from farther away, such as animal hides from Central Asia or silk yarn and textiles from China.

During this same period the Chinese started to hear about the commercial exchanges in the "sea market" along India's western coast. By the first century C.E. Chinese silk had become popular among Roman citizens. It was at this time that the Roman naturalist Pliny (ca. 23–79 C.E.) complained about oriental luxuries, including silks, draining Roman treasuries. Fragments of silk damask found in tombs at the ancient trade center of Palmyra in Syria attracted the attention of many modern textile experts, but Otto Maenchen-Helfen was the first to identify these fragments as Han Chinese silk weaving, thus establishing the first material evidence of Han China's silk trade with the Roman Empire.[18]

Despite frequent material exchanges, Romans and Han Chinese probably never had substantial direct contact with each other. In part, this was probably due to the hostility between the Roman Empire and the Persians during the time of the Parthian Empire (the Persians did not want to see any direct contact between China and the Romans). Most of the Chinese goods destined for Rome were transported through the Kushan Empire, which ruled most parts of northern India and a large portion of Central Asia in the early centuries of the common era. The Kushan state controlled almost all the overland routes between the borders of China and the ports on India's western coast. With access to Chinese goods through Central Asia and to India's "sea market," which was linked to the Mediterranean world, luxury goods naturally coursed through Kushan territory.

THE SILK ROAD THROUGH KUSHAN INDIA

The establishment of the Kushan Empire was in part a consequence of the migration of nomadic groups across Asia. Kushana was the name of a tribe under the Yuezhi confederacy. Ancestors of the Yuezhi had once lived in the eastern part of Chinese Central Asia, but they had migrated and settled in Bactria and could not be persuaded to settle accounts with the nomadic Xiongnu federation. Bactria was a fertile land and a highly urbanized region, where the rulers of Achaemenid Persia and the Hellenistic Seleucids had left many cultural legacies. Around 128 B.C.E.

the Great Yuezhi tribe, pressed by the Xiongnu, had driven away the Scythians, who had occupied Bactria before them. At this stage there were five tribes under the Yuezhi confederacy, either original Yuezhi or Scythians who accepted their suzerainty.[19] Kushana, one of these five tribes, unified the tribes into a kingdom. King Kujula Kadphises took control of Central Asian territory from Samarkand in the north to Panjishir in the south. From his capital city of Bactra (modern-day Balkh in northern Afghanistan), he crossed the Hindu Kush in 50 C.E. and conquered the greater part of both Afghanistan and Gandhara (in modern-day northwestern Pakistan). His successors pushed Kushan territory further into what is now India. The most well-known Kushan ruler was Kanishka, though historians are still not sure about his dates.[20] During the time of Kanishka, perhaps in the first century C.E., the Kushan Empire included much of Central Asia and northern India, and its political center moved from Purushapura (modern-day Peshawar, in northwestern Pakistan) to Mathura on the banks of the Yamuna River, a tributary of the Ganges.[21]

The extensive territory of the Kushan Empire and its frequent contact with China provided abundant resources for the Kushans to trade with the Romans. In the early centuries of the common era, the ports of western India — Barbaricum and Barygaza — were probably not under the direct control of the Kushans, at least not for the entire period. Rather, these ports were sometimes controlled by the western Shakas, newcomers to South Asia from West or Central Asia. Nevertheless, since the Kushans had under their control most of the commodities demanded by the Romans — such as Chinese silks, Central Asian furs, precious stones and spices from the mountainous areas of Afghanistan and the Himalayas — Roman goods, upon arriving at western Indian ports, easily found their way to the Kushan regime's core region in northwestern India and further inner Asia.

This has been verified by archaeological finds in Begram, a village in Afghanistan.[22] Begram was the site of the royal city of the Kushan king Kadphises, as well as the summer residence for Kushan rulers after the capital moved to Mathura on the hot Indian plain. In one room of the palace, probably where a treasury had been, archaeologists found an enormous collection of exotic wares from China, India, and the Mediterranean, representing an accumulation of more than 150 years. French archaeologists did detailed comparative studies to verify the provenance of various art works.[23] The lacquer vessels from China, exquisite ivory carvings from India, and the sculptures, glass vessels, and other art works from the Roman Empire were probably tribute given by traders and caravans that passed through Kushan territory.

When the Kushans established rule in northern India, they still possessed some features of a horse-riding people. The headless stone statue of Kanishka found in Mathura shows apparel and physical features of a steppe people: high boots, belted tunics, and feet with toes pointing outward. It was under the rule of these former nomads that Central Asia and northern India experienced an age of unprecedented urban prosperity. Many urban centers appeared in Afghanistan, Central Asia, and in what is now northern Pakistan. In the area of modern-day India, Mathura and Ujjain were probably the largest metropolitan areas. Mathura was surrounded by many satellite towns that facilitated transportation and communication around the region.

Archaeological excavations have revealed great building activities at the levels occupied by the Kushans in these urban sites. Large red burnt bricks were characteristic Kushan building materials. Many ordinary houses, not only the palaces or large edifices, were built with this kind of brick, and many had more than one storey. The material wealth of urban life was at least in part the result of a flourishing trade, both domestic trade inside the Kushan territory and intercultural long-distance trade. The profusion of commercial activities was also reflected in Kushan art, which was mostly Buddhist. This dominance begs the question of Buddhism's role in Eurasian trade, and more specifically, in the trade along the Silk Road, as well as an examination of the impact of Silk Road trade on the development of Buddhism.

$$\boxed{2}$$

Buddhism and the Silk Road

Wʜᴇɴ ᴛʜᴇ Bᴜᴅᴅʜᴀ ᴛᴀᴜɢʜᴛ ʜɪs ᴅᴏᴄᴛʀɪɴᴇs ᴀɴᴅ ᴏʀɢᴀɴɪᴢᴇᴅ ᴍᴏɴᴀsᴛɪᴄ orders (*sanghas*) during the sixth and fifth centuries ʙ.ᴄ.ᴇ., northern India was experiencing a second period of urbanization. Its first period of urbanization had taken place along the Indus River, where the cities of the Harappan civilization (named after one of its major urban sites) flourished during the third and second millennia ʙ.ᴄ.ᴇ. Most of the cities during the second period of urbanization were located around the middle or lower Ganges plain. Buddha, the *muni* or sage of the Shakya Republic, often traveled to and gave his sermons in cities such as Rajagriha, Sravasti, and Vaisali. Except for metropolitan Taxila, the northwestern region was quite rustic in comparison with the Ganges plain, and the Buddha himself never set foot in the northwestern area. By the time the Kushans ruled northern India, however, the northwest had become the political and economic core of South Asia. Buddhist institutions flourished in the northwest, Kushan kings patronized Buddhism, and as a result many legends about and relics of the Buddha in this area appeared there.

During the early centuries of the common era, Buddhist monasteries developed into institutions far larger, more affluent, and much more complex than the earlier sanghas. Buddhist theology also became far more complicated than the pristine teachings of the Buddha had been. Among the many Buddhist schools of that time, Mahayana Buddhism became the most prevalent. Two mutually dependent features that distinguished it from earlier Buddhism should be mentioned. First, nihilism, the concept of "emptiness" (that is, the objects people see or feel do not exist; rather, they are only illusions of the subject), was embodied in earlier forms of Buddhism. The Mahayana school of thought pushed this concept even further. Mahayana texts tended to treat everything as meaningless or nonexisting. Not only did the objects of observation not exist, but the observers themselves did not exist either. Second, ironically, this philosophy that absolutely denied the material world emerged at a time when Buddhist institutions were unprecedentedly wealthy, just like the surrounding society. So far there have been only a few pieces of evidence suggesting that Buddhist monasteries actively participated in trade, but abundant evidence shows that they did receive large amounts of material patronage from traders, artisans, and other urban dwellers. The numerous votive inscriptions dated to the Kushan period attest to the material patronage to Buddhist monasteries.[1] In the time of the Buddha, monks had to beg for food on a daily basis, but during the Kushan period most monasteries set out a large symbolic begging bowl to receive donations in the form of coins and precious items.

The wealth that flowed into the monasteries not only produced marvelous art works in and on cave temples, on monumental stupas (giant mounts containing relics of the Buddha) and their surrounding railings, and on monastic walls and buildings, but this wealth also changed monasteries into economic entities. Monasteries had to trade the donated valuables for provisions in order to maintain the monks. Monastic establishments also took the lead in large construction projects, including monasteries and stupas. They had to coordinate the individual donations of single pieces of art into a much larger design. Buddhist sculptures were often the donations of individuals, as shown by inscriptions revealing the names and titles of the donors and indicating what blessings they hoped to receive in return. Nevertheless, the sculptures became inseparable constituent parts of a much larger complex of monumental structures.

BUDDHISM AND MATERIAL CULTURE

In contrast to the asceticism that Buddhist monks were supposed to observe, Buddhist art at this time depicted lively urban life. From Central Asia to northern India, sculptures and murals in monastic settings depicted multilevel buildings, musicians and acrobats, women holding mirrors for applying makeup, people peeking out of windows or balconies to observe activities on the streets, and drinking, even many bacchanalian drinking parties.

There were two major schools of Buddhist art during the Kushan period. Gandharan art developed in northwestern India and reflected the influence of Persian and Hellenistic rule in that region.[2] The Mathuran school was more indigenous to India. Themes and details of both schools show the obvious impact of the Roman trade, however. One interesting example is that in most of the drinking scenes, the vessels are Roman-style, high-footed goblets. No matter how Buddhologists explain this interesting phenomenon, such art works testify to the proximity, perhaps even involvement, of Buddhist institutions in urban, commercial life.

Sculptures were not the only expressions of devotion in Buddhist monastic art. In those days stupas may not have been the bare stone structures that are evident today. Rather, they were probably heavily decorated with valuables. The famous Dharmarajika stupa in Taxila was surrounded by a pavement of glass tiles.[3] Excavations around the stupas also reveal scattered piles or hoards of glass beads, pearls, corals, or precious stones. These same stupas were perhaps also decorated with silk festoons, as indicated by the draping decorations carved on miniature stupas or in relief depicting stupas. The Buddhist sanghas were no longer congregations of modest mendicants but institutions unabashedly displaying their material wealth.

The seeming incompatibility between metaphysical discussions of the nonexistence of things and the indulgence in mundane material life is fully displayed in some Buddhist Sanskrit texts, a new genre of Buddhist literature that developed along with Mahayana thought. A typical example was the Mahayana text *Saddharmapundarika* (The Lotus Sutra). The early part of the text develops the idea that the wisdom of the Buddha is hard to obtain, that only the Buddha himself knows all.[4] The text claims the emptiness of all dharmas (doctrines), including Buddhist ones, and that the true dharma is beyond understanding.[5] Because most Buddhist devotees would not be able to obtain the supreme knowledge, the *Lotus Sutra* recommended conversion through supernatural power, including that of talismanic charms.[6]

Building and worshipping stupas for relics of the Buddha and making donations to the Buddha became the most effective means to achieving enlightenment. In the text of the *Lotus Sutra*, the Buddha demanded that his devotees make 84,000 stupas for him, and inside the stupas there should be reliquaries (receptacles for displaying or housing sacred relics) decorated with the "seven treasures." The stupas should be decorated with silk bands and bells, canopies or banners, and devotees should worship the Buddhas and bodhisattvas[7] routinely with gifts of flowers, incense, garlands, ointments, clothes, necklaces, gems and jewels, canopies, flags, and banners.[8] Those items together with the seven treasures and silks were not only common urban consumption goods at that time, but they were also the most common commodities found in the long-distance trade on the Silk Road. The seven treasures—interpreted variously as gold, silver, lapis lazuli, red coral, crystal, pearls, agate or some other precious stones – along with silk decorations are frequently mentioned in many Mahayana Buddhist texts of this period. They were seen in representations of the Buddha lands and heavens, and they were required for all kinds of ritual occasions, as they were the very symbols of Buddhist sacredness and purity. Since then, the concept of the seven treasures has permeated Buddhist literature and their colors are frequently displayed in Buddhist art. Even the hair of the Buddha was described and depicted with the sky blue of lapis lazuli.

A close examination of those ritual items serves as a reminder to us that some of them came from afar, while others were what India was famous for. Red coral came from the eastern Mediterranean, which is the major supplier of this jewel even today. It was a commodity much in demand in both South Asia and China. Crystal, lapis lazuli, and pearls were products that South Asian countries exported both westerly to the Mediterranean world and easterly to China. Silk, of course, was China's most demanded commodity.

The essential role of the seven treasures and silks in Buddhist rituals made those luxuries not only expensive but also sacred, thus necessary. Buddhist devotees, whether rich or poor – be they monks, nuns, or lay people – would exhaust their means to purchase some of these treasures to express their devotion so that they might reach enlightenment. Archaeological finds in Central Asia, China, and India verify this expression of devotion by Buddhists. On the site of the Dharmarajika stupa and monastery in Taxila, excavators found many of these precious items. Chinese literature records coral as a product of the Roman Empire, and coral beads were found at later Buddhist sites in China, as were pearls and glass vessels and beads, a substitute for lapis lazuli or crystal.

BUDDHISM AND TRADE

Although the Kushan Empire was one of the major beneficiaries of the Silk Road, it did not last very long. By the mid-third century C.E. it had shrunk to a small kingdom attached to Persia's rising Sassanian Empire (ca. 224–651 C.E.). Soon the many prosperous urban centers in northwestern India became desolate. The decline of the Kushan Empire, however, was not the only cause (nor even the main cause) of the decline of this section of the Silk Road. With China's fall into political chaos after the demise of the Han Empire in the early third century, with the crises and disintegration of the Roman Empire that started in the fourth century, coupled with the rise of Christianity as a religious institution, the dimensions and directions of trade along the Silk Road underwent a series of changes.

Despite the demise of the Han and the Kushans, the traffic of silk and other luxuries through Central Asia continued. Now traders not only had to undertake the physically difficult journey through Central Asia, but they also had to deal with perilous political situations such as the post-Han warfare in China. Kharoshthi letters dated to the third century C.E. from Shanshan on the Silk Road noted that traders were arriving from China.[9] Travels of Sogdian merchants and Buddhist preachers and pilgrims indicate that the Central Asian routes were viable in the following centuries.[10] Persistence of the trade in luxuries along the Central Asian routes indicates that the demand of ruling elites in both China and India did not diminish, despite the fact that political regimes changed frequently. More important, perhaps, was that Buddhist theology and proselytizing stimulated the demand for the luxuries.

As mentioned above, scholars have learned that the luxuries traded along the Silk Road had been codified as sacred symbols of devotion in Mahayana Buddhist texts. The sacredness attached to those originally mundane goods actually stimulated and, to a certain extent, sustained the trade in luxuries in a period not suitable for long-distance trade. It was during the Kushan period, when Buddhist institutions flourished and became affluent, that Buddhist theology developed along lines that proved to be a stimulus to missionary activities outside India. In the pantheon of Mahayana Buddhism, numerous bodhisattvas (who could reach the state of bliss imminently) chose instead to stay outside the threshold in order to help others across the darkness. With the material strength of monasteries and missionary zeal, Buddhism reached China around the mid-first century C.E. But for a long time Buddhism remained a religion important only within communities of foreign traders, mostly those from Kushan territory, who had some lay Chinese followers. After the fall of the Han, during a period of warfare and political disintegration, however, Buddhism gained influence in China and became the predominant religion there.

Among the various Buddhist schools taught in China, Mahayana was the most successful. Many important Mahayana texts, including the *Lotus Sutra*, had been translated into Chinese in the post-Han period. During the third and fourth centuries, the construction of Buddhist cave temples, statues, and stupas gained momentum. The process reached its apex during the Northern Dynasties period (439–581 C.E.). There were 6,478 officially registered monasteries in northern China in 477 C.E., and more than thirty thousand in 534 C.E.[11] In the Northern Wei capital of Pingcheng, there were about one hundred monasteries in 477 C.E., and the number reached 1,376 in its new capital of Loyang in 534 C.E.[12] The rulers of northern China during those centuries had been mostly nomadic in the recent past. They patronized Buddhism, a foreign religion, rather than indigenous Confucianism or Taoism, since they themselves were foreign. Under the patronage of both state and commercial communities, Chinese Buddhist institutions became extremely rich in a relatively short period.

Monasteries lavishly decorated stupas with luxuries obtained locally or from afar. At least in their religious practices Chinese Buddhists strictly followed the instructions of the *Lotus Sutra* and other Mahayana texts. Contemporary descriptions of Buddhist stupas and festival occasions, as well as archaeological finds, suggest that Buddhist monasteries were probably the largest consumers of such luxuries in China.

Meanwhile, Chinese silks continued to be in demand in India despite the disintegration of the Kushan Empire and a decline of urban centers in northwestern India. In the fourth century the kings of the Gupta dynasty (ca. 320–550 C.E.) reorganized the political structure of northern India by bringing many small kingdoms and tribes under their control or suzerainty. The center of political power in northern India, however, shifted back to the middle and lower Ganges valley. While trading activities and urban culture, including Buddhist institutions, withered in northwestern regions, Buddhist monasteries and commercial economy in the middle and lower Ganges valley continued to flourish for several centuries thereafter.

Chinese silks are mentioned in the Sanskrit literature of this period. Silk banners and hangings were indispensable for Buddhist ceremonies, as witnessed by the Chinese pilgrim Faxian, who was in India from 405 to 411 C.E. Buddhist devotees donated silk decorations to monasteries and used them in parades. A century later, on a pilgrimage to India, the Chinese pilgrims Songyun and Huisheng saw a stupa near Khotan in Central Asia decorated with several tens of thousands of silk banners, and more than half were from their homeland, the kingdom of the Northern Wei in China.[13] The two pilgrims, envoys of the Northern Wei royalty, carried with them one thousand banners of colored silk about thirty meters long, and five hundred silk incense bags, plus two thousand small banners.[14] Songyun and Huisheng donated these silk textiles to Buddhist institutions along the way to India. As the monasteries on the routes often provided lodging and provisions for missionaries and pilgrims, their donations could be considered as a form of exchange. Silk was indeed the most prevalent currency and an important form of property in Central Asia. Until the Tang dynasty (618–906 C.E.) unified China in the seventh century, the trade route between India and China via Central Asia was probably the Silk Road's most active section.

3

Silk Producers outside China

Dᴜʀɪɴɢ ᴛʜɪs sᴀᴍᴇ ᴘᴇʀɪᴏᴅ (ᴛʜᴇ ᴛʜɪʀᴅ ᴛʜʀᴏᴜɢʜ ᴛʜᴇ sᴇᴠᴇɴᴛʜ ᴄᴇɴᴛᴜʀɪᴇs), trading activities between the Mediterranean world and East Asia, through Iran or India, also underwent fundamental changes. First, China was no longer the only country weaving beautiful, elaborate silk textiles, although the technology of producing long and shiny silk filament took a few more centuries to become common knowledge outside China. Central Asian oasis peoples, located on the Silk Road and close to China, started sericulture and silk weaving in the fourth century C.E. at the latest. India produced abundant silk textiles, but because the silk yarn came from a different species of worm and was processed by a technology different from that of China, they could not compete with the Chinese product outside South Asia. Sassanid Persia produced polychrome silk fabrics, especially those woven with golden threads. The fame of such textiles reached westward to Gaul in the fifth century[1] and eastward to China in the sixth century.[2] The Sassanian style was so popular that both its designs and weaving technique influenced silk weaving in the Tang Empire of China.[3]

Sɪʟᴋ Wᴇᴀᴠɪɴɢ Usɪɴɢ Cʜɪɴᴇsᴇ Yᴀʀɴ

Silk weaving with Chinese yarn started in the eastern Mediterranean cities of Antioch, Berytus, Tyre, and possibly Gaza during the Roman period. Under the Byzantine Empire silk weaving flourished to the extent that competition with Persia for materials became fierce. The Byzantine emperor Justinian I (ruled 527–65 C.E.) allied with the Ethiopian kingdom of Axum, hoping to get around Persia's monopoly of silk materials.[4] The Chinese also started to realize that the demand for silk abroad was mostly for silk materials, not necessarily the finished textiles. Historical literature dated to the fourth or fifth century refers to the fact that the Romans really only wanted silk yarn.[5] And some later documents note that the Romans unraveled plain Chinese silk cloth for the threads to make patterned silk textiles.[6]

The development of silk weaving outside China gradually changed the nature of silk as a commodity and the pattern of its circulation. Unlike the plain tabby silks, patterned silk-compound textiles were not the products of the rural household economy. They not only required much more work for dying and designing, but they also demanded a more complicated division of labor and sophisticated instruments and technology. These textiles could only be produced in highly organized urban-based workshops or state-owned workshops. While plain or colored tabby silks continued to flow out of China along the Silk Road, without much obstruction, high-quality silks with artistic designs started to become a rare commodity on the Silk Road, even though they were produced in quantity in various silk centers of Eurasia.

MONOPOLIES OF BYZANTIUM AND TANG CHINA

Fancy silk textiles became hard to obtain because both the Byzantine Empire and the Tang Empire established sumptuary codes that limited who could wear what sorts of silk textiles. Following the short-lived Sui dynasty, which unified China in 589 C.E., the Tang dynasty began to draw up a comprehensive clothing code for its court soon after it took power in 618. This code was designed to mark differences of status in the bureaucracy. While the emperors reserved for themselves the right to wear yellow, the traditional supreme color, the color purple was reserved for the highest officials—a major departure from the traditional view of color status. Confucius had denounced purple as an impure variation of a true red, but during the Tang Empire, even the emperors' daily robes were purple, although yellow robes were still used for ritual occasions. Various designs on colored silk textiles, such as animal motifs, realistic or abstract, were also assigned to different levels of officials. Sophisticated textiles and clothing could only be made in government workshops, under strict supervision. Anyone else who dared to make or sell those items risked harsh punishment.

Meanwhile, Byzantine emperors established a similar kind of clothing code. In the process of consolidating his power, Justinian I managed to crush the private silk-weaving industry by monopolizing all silk materials. In the following centuries Byzantines gradually established sericulture. When the supply of silk materials became abundant, the purple dye and weaving technique of patterned silks became the key to government control of high-quality silks. The combination of silk and purple dye became the core of the Byzantine silk monopoly. Purple was a costly dyestuff extracted from murex, a shellfish found in the eastern Mediterranean. Roman citizens who could afford it had been able to obtain purple, but under the increasingly absolutist rule of the Byzantine regime, purple became the very symbol of royalty and religious sacredness.[7] From the mid-fourth to the early fifth century the empire issued a series of sumptuary laws that denied commoners the right to wear purple silks and silk textiles woven with gold threads. In addition to the sumptuary laws, the Code of Justinian also regulated the production of purple dye and silk.[8] Precious purple silk textiles and robes became the symbol of royal prestige, a material representative of Roman culture, and thus a useful weapon for diplomacy.[9]

Neither the Byzantine rulers nor the Chinese emperors willingly gave up their monopoly of precious silks, but the monopolies nevertheless fell apart. The Tang dynasty collapsed in 906 C.E., and subsequent dynasties never enacted sumptuary laws. In Europe, from the ninth or tenth century, Byzantine silks were no longer the only choice available, and silk textiles, including the most fancy weavings, became a commodity around the Mediterranean. Among the many factors and forces that contributed to the breakdown of these monopolies and to changes that transformed silk into a real commodity, the most important were religious—Buddhist, Christian, Islamic, and others.

4

Contributions of Religious Activities

IN LATE ANTIQUITY AND EARLY MEDIEVAL TIMES RELIGIOUS FUNCTIONS WERE the most prominent activities, and religious piety was the most respected feeling in many societies of Eurasia. Commercial activities such as trading and money lending were often considered to be unrespectable professions. Religious activities and material transactions, however, were often intrinsically mixed together. Religious beliefs frequently affected or even decided the pattern of social behavior, including the ways of acquiring, accumulating, and spending wealth. Because religious beliefs and functions were often shared by all social levels—both by rulers and the ruled, the poor and the rich—religious institutions and ideology could channel the surplus of a society in a certain direction.

In the context of Buddhism, as previously discussed, proselytizing in Central Asia and China and the designation of certain commodities in the long-distance trade as sacred had helped to sustain the transactions between India and China when the overall environment was not favorable to trade. Over the centuries, as Buddhist institutions and theology continued to evolve in India, their influence on Chinese and other Asian peoples became increasingly profound, and they created a totally different vision of the cosmos and the afterlife. Although Confucius did not provide a clear picture of the afterlife, Chinese rulers and even commoners sought to bring as much worldly wealth as possible with them to their graves. Evidence of this practice is the large-scale human sacrifices of the bronze age and the terracotta troops of Shi Huangdi (ruled 221–210 B.C.E.), known as the First Emperor, whose tomb was filled with thousands of life-size terracotta horses and soldiers. The Buddhist concepts of the transmigration of souls and of karma—that after death the soul of one creature would be born into another, and that one's behavior in former lives would determine the conditions of the new life—changed the popular beliefs about the world, heaven, and hell. The crucial point is that the wealth one could carry into one's future lives was not material but meritorious, evidence of good deeds done in former lives. This concept penetrated into every level of Chinese society and into the theology of other religions. By the time of the Tang dynasty, whether rulers or commoners, whether Buddhists or not, Chinese shared a fear of hell and a hope for a better future life. And because Mahayana Buddhism encouraged devotion and donation as a way to gain merits, the material wealth of this life could be transformed into the wealth of future lives through the mediation of Buddhist institutions.

Both literary evidence and archaeological finds demonstrate that more and more wealth flowed into Buddhist institutions in Central Asia, China, and India. Many of the donations, including silk textiles and clothing, were major components of the wealth stored under stupas, along with relics of the Buddha. But there were also many silks that became transactional goods for monks and monasteries, and thus were introduced into circulation by religious institutions. Tang rulers and high officials often donated wealth to support Buddhist monastic construction and maintenance, often in the form of silk textiles and clothing, and often of the forbidden types (according to sumptuary laws). They rewarded Buddhist priests—Chinese or foreign, often Indian—with thousands of bolts and pieces of silk textiles and honorary robes for their religious services. The ranking of the honorary robes was similar to that of the bureaucracy, excluding the imperial yellow. Therefore the highest rank of ritual robes was purple, perhaps with golden embroidery.

More Buddhist pilgrims continued the tradition of carrying silks donated by their patrons to India, on an even larger scale. The famous Chinese pilgrim Xuanzang, who went to India in 630, received a large quantity of silks and other wealth from one of his patrons, the king of Gaochang, en route to Central Asia in modern-day Turpan (in the northwestern part of the Tarim basin). Xuanzang needed thirty horses and twenty-five laborers to carry all the treasures.[1] And one Tang ruler sent an envoy to Kapisa in 661 to purchase a piece of the Buddha's bone with four thousand bolts of silk.[2] Tang emperors continuously sent envoys carrying precious honorary robes to spread on the Buddha's throne in the Mahabodhi monastery in Bodh Gaya, where the Buddha reached enlightenment. Carrying silk textiles and robes to India, pilgrims earned merits for both their patrons and themselves.

CHRISTIANITY AND THE CULT OF SAINTS

In the western part of Eurasia a similar demand for silk textiles evolved because of developments in the Christian religion. More specifically, Christian eschatology and the cult of saints sustained the demand for silks.[3] In Roman times funerals had been a showcase of family wealth and fame. The Franks also buried their precious items with the dead. A clear vision of the structure of the world beyond emerged in the late fourth century.[4] The Christian concept of the afterlife—hell, purgatory, heaven, and the last judgment—gradually changed the custom of burying wealth with the dead. Early Christian priests tried to convince people that no matter how well the dead were dressed, they would still meet their maker naked. Although such efforts to carry material wealth to the afterworld were futile, according to Christian clergy, donating wealth to the churches and to cover tombs or reliquaries of saints would be fruitful. In time, burials of commoners became simpler, and more and more treasures went to the tombs of saints, priests, and kings, as priests and kings were considered to be potential saints. From the sixth century silk covers on tombs became the indicator of canonized saints.[5]

The cult of saints soon reached a new height. In the early centuries of Christianity, saints were rarely disturbed in their tombs, neither the martyrs in Rome nor local saints in western Europe. By the seventh century or perhaps earlier, however, Christians began to dig up relics of saints and transfer them to various churches in Europe. Although many early churches had been built on the tombs of saints, possession of a saint's relic now became the necessary condition for building new churches. Reliquaries became the very treasuries of the churches, because the saints attracted donations from the devotees. At that time, kings, bishops, and Christian commoners all wanted to be buried close to the saints for their own salvation. Usually, ordinary Christians had to stay in the churchyards, whereas kings and high priests might be able to squeeze into the church itself. Their bodies and tombs were covered with the most exquisite silks, similar to those used for saints.

Thus many beautiful silk samples found their way to all parts of Europe from the Byzantine Empire, Persia, and even Central Asia. More than a thousand silk samples dated from the seventh to the twelfth centuries that were preserved in western European churches have been cataloged. Most of them are Byzantine, and there are a few Persian-Islamic silks, but only one is a noticeably Chinese-patterned silk sample.[6] In the sphere of Christendom the movement of exquisite silks was closely associated with pilgrimage and was often in response to demand caused by religious functions. Thus most silks circulated basically within this religious sphere.

Byzantine authorities were loathe to let some of their good silk textiles leave their territory. As late as the tenth century, when Liudprand, the bishop of Cremona, went to Constantinople as an envoy of Otto I, Byzantine custom officers arrogantly confiscated his purchase of purple silks. In vain, Liudprand protested that the silks were for his church, and that they could be purchased from Venetian and Amalfian traders in the market of Pavia anyway.[7] Christians in western Europe had to resort to other sources to meet the demand of their religious functions.

SILK FROM THE ISLAMIC REGION

Western Europe's most important alternative source of silk was the Islamic region, where silk production and trade were political and commercial activities as well as religious. After the first military confrontation between Muslim and Chinese forces at Talas in Central Asia in 751 C.E., the Arabs did not force their luck further eastward. They did take away many Chinese captives, however, including paper makers and silk weavers and dyers. Under the Islamic regimes sericulture and filature techniques that produced long filaments of silk yarn spread from Central Asia all the way to the western Mediterranean. Islamic states also took over many silk workshops in the newly conquered lands, especially in the former Sassanian and Byzantine territories. As many of these workshops had been subject to government regulation, the caliphs of the early Islamic empire established what was known as the *tiraz* system to suit their own needs. Under this system, textiles produced in tiraz workshops—whether silk, cotton, or linen—carried inscriptions of Islamic religious messages and the date of the regime. The inscriptions were tapestried or embroidered with silk threads.

The tiraz institution served Islamic regimes by making their powers known to their subjects through one of the most common media. With the development of sericulture, tiraz factories produced large quantities of silk and half-silk textiles, in addition to the cheaper materials, linen and cotton. Because there were no sumptuary laws against commoners wearing silks in any of the Islamic regions, the silk industry flourished, and silk yarn and textiles became common commodities.[8] Muslim and Jewish traders freely traded silk throughout the Mediterranean region. Meanwhile, European Christians were so eager to obtain silks for their saints, many of the Islamic textiles found their way to churches. That those silks were treasured as much as Byzantine silks is testified to by the fact that during the early Renaissance, tiraz inscriptions praising Allah in Persian or Arabic appeared on the portraits of Mary and other Christian sacred figures.[9]

Even the Islamic production could not keep up with the growth of Christian demand, however. Liturgical garments for priests, hangings and decorations for churches and cathedrals, and coverings for saints became more and more elaborate. As a result, Christians in Italy, the Frankish kingdoms, and England started to make liturgical silks by embroidering plain silks. Embroidery enabled them to make silks for donations to churches without benefit of the complicated technology of the drawlooms that wove patterned silks. The embroidered pieces could be as beautiful and as precious as those with woven patterns, if not more so.

Embroidery would become popular, however, only because silk material and textiles were more available, due to a number of factors. At least until the Song dynasty (960–1279 C.E.), plain silks never stopped flowing out of China, carried by Central Asian nomads and traders. The Islamic conquests did not stop this flow. Instead, the silk industry and sericulture increased the supply, which slackened Byzantium's monopoly and ushered in a new age in the silk trade.

5

Nomads and Central Asian Traders

DURING THE PERIOD THAT THE BYZANTINE EMPIRE AND TANG CHINA tried to maintain their monopolies of exquisite silk textiles, silk yarn and plain silk textiles had never been subject to restrictions. As previously discussed, the production and circulation of plain silk had increased substantially and helped to undermine the monopoly of both the Tang and the Byzantine Empires. Nevertheless, it is difficult to identify the circulation routes using literary records and surviving samples because plain silk and silk yarn were not as exotic as the colorful compound weavings and were therefore less noticed. The spread of sericulture and filature technology certainly provided new sources of silk supply outside China after 751 C.E. However, there is no doubt that Chinese production of silk yarn and plain silk textiles also increased greatly during the Tang Empire. This increase was due in part to the flourishing Tang economy, of which silk production was a major component. At least since the Han dynasty, plain silk textiles and silk yarn had been an essential part of household production and a major form of tax paid to the government, and thus the main stock in the state treasuries. Increases in population and agricultural production in general certainly led to increased silk tax revenues paid to the state. At the same time, the foreign demand for silk and the high prices that it fetched in foreign markets probably also stimulated its production. A Tang writer, You Du (735–812 C.E.), made it clear that what the Romans (actually, the Christian market) wanted from

China, instead of fancy silk textiles, was silk yarn or plain silk textiles that they could unravel to make "damask and patterned silk of dark red color."[1]

HORSE-SILK EXCHANGES

As for the Tang rulers' interest in this trade, the foreign demand for silk was less of a motivating factor than their own desire for foreign goods. Good horses, which had enticed the Han emperor Wudi to send military expeditions to Central Asia, were still the major items traded for Chinese silks. Because China's agricultural society was virtually totally dependent on the "Western Regions" and the steppe to supply its major draft animals, the horse-silk trade was one of the main trading activities of Tang China.

During the entire Tang dynasty, many peoples went to China to obtain large quantities of plain silk and silk yarn, and they were often involved in horse-silk exchanges. During the time of the Sassanid Empire (226–651 C.E.), Zoroastrian Persians were frequent traders in China. Soon after it consolidated its regime, the Tang administration set up a special office to deal with Persian-Zoroastrian affairs.[2] This office was called *Sabao*, a Chinese transliteration of the Sanskrit *sarthavaha*, the word for a caravan leader. Zoroastrian temples, which also functioned as mercantile centers for Persian traders, were located near the market places in Chinese cities and along the trade routes.

In competition with the Persians were Turks who then lived in Central Asia. Those Turks, who were nomads, did not produce silk but engaged in trade, selling horses to the Chinese and silks to the west. In the sixth century a Turkish ruler sent an envoy, a Sogdian trader, to the court of Justin II (ruled 565–74 C.E.) in Constantinople to make an alliance against the Persians to guarantee the arrival of west-bound silks.[3]

Both Persians and Turks employed Sogdians as their agents. Ancient Sogdiana (now a part of Uzbekistan, and the locale of Bukhara and Samarkand) flourished as a result of its good agricultural lands and its strategic location on Eurasian trade routes. Sogdian merchants seemed to be willing to adopt any religion to suit their commercial activities. They were propagators of Buddhism in China from the second to the fourth centuries C.E., while engaged in the early phase of the silk trade. After the expansion of the Sassanid Empire in Iran, these Sogdian merchants became Zoroastrian, along with the Persians. Thereafter they were known as Manichaeans and worked as trade agents for the Turkish Uighurs. In the Sogdian homeland of Panjikent, murals in a granary owner's home show a hierarchy of family patron deities. The image of Buddha occupies only a small corner. Paintings throughout the room reveal the universalistic approach of the Sogdian people at that time.[4]

The relationship between Sogdian merchants and the Uighurs started with the silk trade. During the eighth century, the Uighurs rose from a tribe to a powerful nomadic state. They helped the Tang government to suppress the mid-eighth century rebellions of the military commanders An Lushan and Shi Siming. In return, the Uighurs received many luxuries from the Tang court and thus began a large-scale horse-silk trade arrangement. Tang records show that on an annual basis the Uighurs obtained one million bolts of plain silk textiles in return for the payment of one hundred thousand horses.[5] One million bolts of silk was a substantial portion of Tang revenue, because in the mid-eighth century — the golden age of the Tang imperial economy — the annual revenue of silk for the empire was about 7,400,000 bolts.[6] Obviously, the Uighurs did not consume all those silks by themselves. To make a profit, they relied on Sogdian traders to take them west to sell.[7] In the process, the Uighurs adopted the religion of the Sogdians, which at that time was Manichaeism.

Because the Uighurs frequently went to Tang China to trade, they built the first Manichaean monastery there in 768. More were built in major trading cities and along the trade routes during the following decades.[8] As in the case of the Zoroastrians, the temples were not only religious centers for Uighurs and Sogdians but also storehouses for commodities. In the early ninth century the Uighurs and the Tang rulers had such a close relationship that a Tang princess married the Uighur ruler. Soon, however, tension built up between them. The Uighurs considered themselves to be the protectors of the Tang regime and had high expectations with regard to what the dynasty owed them. The Tang government was embarrassed by not being able to make overdue silk payments for horses, claiming the prices were extraordinarily high and the number of horses was too large for the Chinese market. Having suffered a military defeat at the hands of the Kirghiz in 840 and struck by a famine about the same time, the Uighurs were desperate to get their payments for the horses. Unable to obtain the silks and food that they had been promised, the Uighurs started to loot Chinese settlements along Tang borders. A war finally broke out, and the Tang princess returned home. In 843 the Tang government ordered the confiscation of all the property of Manichaean monasteries. Two years later the Tang ruler issued orders to banish all foreign religious institutions in China, thus ending the most tolerant and cosmopolitan era in premodern Chinese history.[9]

Because of its deep roots in China, Buddhism quickly recovered from persecution, and Manichaeism went underground. Nevertheless, in the eighty-some years of the Uighur-Tang alliance, large quantities of plain silk flowed out of China in a westerly direction as a result of the horse-silk trade arrangements. Even after the suppression of foreign religions in the Tang Empire and the division and migration of the Uighurs, the horse-silk trade between the Uighurs and the Chinese continued. Because of the dynamics of Central Asian politics, in the process of their migrations the Uighurs then converted to Buddhism. In the tenth or eleventh century, after the Muslim Saljuq Turks from West Asia extended their power to Central Asia, other Turkic peoples, including some Uighurs, converted to Islam. Nomadic Turks had always been hospitable to traders and pilgrims. Now hospitality to traders and caravans was institutionalized by the Islamic state. Saljuq rulers ensured the security of the caravan trade by compensating from state treasuries traders who were robbed in their territory.[10] Turkish states in Central Asia built fortified caravanserais every thirty to forty kilometers along the routes, based on an average day's journey, in order to provide lodging and services.[11]

By this time, however, traders passing through Islamic Central Asia did not deal directly with the Chinese who produced silks, but with the Tanguts, the Khitans, and the Jerchins who occupied China's northern frontiers and exacted the silks from the Song government in the form of tribute or through trade. The quantity traded along the land routes was still substantial, but probably less than that of the Tang period, and less than the quantities that Chinese shippers during the Song dynasty began to carry on the southern sea routes.

SEA ROUTES REPLACED LAND ROUTES

From the ninth century a new market for silk formed in the Mediterranean, and the sea routes linking the Mediterranean to China gradually replaced the land routes as the major channel of long-distance trade. Christians, Jews, Muslims, Nestorians, and Zoroastrians all participated in the silk trade via sea routes.

Despite the battle of Talas in 751, when the Arabs routed the Tang army, the Arab empire and China did have commercial contacts, mostly through sea routes. Based on ports along the southeast coast of China—Canton, Quanzhou (Zayton), and Yangzhou—Muslim traders (both Arabs and Persians) traded in many areas in China. In Chinese folk literature these traders were portrayed as fabulously rich merchants. They supplied Chinese colored silk textile (*firanb*), golden brocade (*kimkhaw*), and more often, silk yarn named after the port Zayton (*zaytuni*) to the Mediterranean market.[12] Jewish traders also went to China, but they were more active in the Mediterranean region, where they traded along with Muslims. Geniza documents show that the Mediterranean market was a haven for traders of various communities since the mid-tenth century, especially for Jewish traders.[13]

On the northern coast of the Mediterranean, Venice and other Italian cities rose as trading centers. Venice, under the sovereignty of Byzantium, was the major broker of Byzantine silks to western Europe.

With its naval superiority, Venice bargained with the weakening Byzantine state about silk supply. Silks were transported to Pavia in Lombardy, then to various parts of Europe. The Byzantines had used silk supply as a weapon to keep Venice and other Italian cities from Frankish overlordship, but Venice managed to gain its autonomy by manipulating in the conflicts between Frankish states and Byzantium and between Islamic and Christian powers, and it finally emerged as a powerful trading and maritime state. In ports on the southern coast, Jewish and Muslim traders donned whatever kind of expensive textiles they pleased, and sold silk textiles from all over Eurasia—from China, Egypt, India, Mesopotamia, Persia, Sicily, and Spain. By this time most Chinese silk yarn in the Mediterranean ports was probably coming from ports in southeastern China, such as Zayton (Quanzhou). According to S. D. Goitein, silk yarn in the Mediterranean market was not only a commodity, but it was also a kind of standard cash, along with gold and silver.[14] This southern sea route eventually overtook the overland routes in importance and became the most important means of communication between the opposite shores of Eurasia.

6

Conclusion

THE REDISCOVERY OF THE SILK ROAD WAS A GREAT EVENT IN ITSELF. NOT only did this event compel Chinese intellectuals during a depressing age to realize the cosmopolitan attitude of their ancestors, but it also reminded scholars around the world that no ancient civilization was totally isolated. In recent years there has been a popular conviction among historians, both Chinese and Western, that Chinese civilization was isolated because the Chinese people, unlike the seafaring Greeks, were inward-looking people. The history of the Silk Road suggests that this assumption is patently wrong. The first emperor of China and Chinese adventurers of his time did try to reach the outside world through the sea, but Japan and other island peoples in the Pacific Ocean had not developed enough to sustain this effort. Once the Han emperor Wudi and his envoy Zhang Qian realized that wealth and culture were located in the West and accessible through the land routes, they unhesitatingly looked westward to the faraway wonderland. Exploring the land routes was neither less dangerous nor less exciting and fruitful than seafaring. In this sense, the mutual reaching out of the West and the East on the Eurasian continent was of no less significance for the ancient world than the discovery of Columbus was for the modern world.

Interactions along the Silk Road involved movements of peoples, materials, and ideas.[1] This essay has focused on the most important material in transaction, silk, and the most important cultural activity, religious exchanges and developments. From the early development of the Silk Road to the time the sea routes replaced land routes, silk trade experienced several major phases, after this changing pattern of silk circulation. During the heyday of the Roman Empire, Chinese silk found its way to the Mediterranean world along with other oriental luxuries, which were traded for exotic goods intended for the Chinese ruling elite.

After the demise of the Han Empire in the third century C.E., when the Roman Empire was also in crisis, silk weaving developed in various parts of Eurasia. Silk trade between China and India persisted, accompanied by the expansion of Buddhist institutions in Asia. In the following centuries, both the Tang and the Byzantine Empires established state monopolies in the production of artistic silk textiles, for establishing bureaucratic and religious hierarchies and for diplomatic maneuver. But Buddhist and Christian religious activities helped to break down the monopolies by channeling the forbidden goods to commoners and thus to the market. Islamic religion and states, and traders of different ethnic and religious backgrounds under Islamic regimes, contributed to the ineffectiveness of sumptuary laws in both empires. The impact of the failure of these laws for the later history of these regions is beyond the scope of this essay. But the dynamic interactions between state and market, religious and secular aspects of life, nomadic and sedentary peoples, town and countryside that were central to the history of the Silk Road can be traced in these important shifts to yet another phase of development.

Notes

1. THE SILK ROAD

1. The controversy of who should keep the art treasures that were taken from Chinese Central Asia is best illustrated in Peter Hopkirk, *Foreign Devils on the Silk Road* (London: John Murray, 1980).

2. Aurel Stein, *Serindia*, 5 vols. (Oxford: Oxford University Press, 1921); and Stein, *Inner Most Asia* (Oxford: Clarendon Press, 1928).

3. Hopkirk, *Foreign Devils*, 111.

4. Albert Grunwedel, *Altbuddhistische Kultstatten in Chinesisch-Turkistan; Bericht uber archaologische Arbeiten von 1906 bis 1907 bei Kuca, Qarasahr und in der oase Turfan* (Berlin: G. Reimer, 1912); Albert von Le Coq, *Buried Treasures of Chinese Turkistan* (London: G. Allen & Unwin Ltd., 1928); W. B. Henning, *Sogdica* (London: Royal Asiatic Society, 1940); A. F. Rudolph Hoernle, *Ancient Manuscripts from Central Asia* (Calcutta, India: Baptist Mission Press, 1897), and *Manuscript Remains of Buddhist Literature Found in Eastern Turkestan* (Oxford: Clarendon Press, 1916); Sten Konow, *Primer of Khotanese Saka: Grammatical Sketch, Chrestomathy, Vocabulary, Bibliography* (Oslo, Norway: H. Aschehoug, W. Nygaard, 1949); Ernst Leumann, *Das Nordarische(sakische) Lehrgedicht des Buddhismus* (Leipzig, Germany: Deutsche morgenlandische gessellschaft, in kommission bei F. A. Brockhaus, 1933–36); Emil Sieg, Wilhelm Siegling, and Werner Thomas, *Tocharische Sprachreste* (Göttingen, Germany: Vandenhoeck & Ruprecht, 1983).

5. Kharoshthi is a script used in northwestern India and part of Central Asia at least since the third century B.C.E. Writing in this script runs from right to left.

6. Thomas Burrow, *A Translation of Kharoshthi Documents from Chinese Turkestan* (London: Royal Asiatic Society, 1940). A Chinese scholar, Lin Meicun, collected additional documents and edited them in Chinese. The first volume of this book was published in 1988 as *Shahai Gujuan* (Ancient documents from the sea of sand) by publisher Wenwu Chubanshe (Beijing). It has not yet been translated from Chinese.

7. Wang Zhongmin, comp., *Dunhuang Guji Xulu* (Beijing: Zhonghua Shuju, 1957).

8. Lionel Giles, *Descriptive Catalogue of the Chinese Manuscripts from Tunhuang in the British Museum* (London: Trustees of the British Museum, 1957).

9. Victor Mair, *T'ang Transformation Text: A Study of the Buddhist Contribution to the Rise of Vernacular Fiction and Drama in China* (Cambridge, Mass.: Council on East Asian Studies, Harvard University; Distributed by Harvard University Press, 1989).

10. For a summary of the event's records by classical writers, see John W. McCrindle, *The Invasion of India by Alexander the Great* (1896; reprint, Delhi: Cosmo Publications, 1983).

11. McCrindle, *Ancient India as Described in Classical Literature* (1901; reprint, New Delhi: Oriental Books, 1979), 26.

12. William H. McNeill, *The Pursuit of Power: Technology, Armed Force, and Society since A.D. 1000* (Chicago: University of Chicago Press, 1982), 6.

13. For scholarship on the Silk Road from the Roman perspective, see Eric Herbert Warmington, *The Commerce between the Roman Empire and India* (1928; reprint, London: Curzon Press, Ltd., 1974); R. E. Mortimer Wheeler, *Rome beyond the Imperial Frontiers* (London: G. Bell & Sons Ltd., 1954). For early maritime trade, including Indian Ocean trade, from the Indian perspective, see Himanshu P. Ray, *The Winds of Change: Buddhism and the Maritime Links of Early South Asia* (Delhi: Oxford University Press, 1994).

14. Lionel Casson, trans. and ed., *The Peripulus Maris Erythraei* (Princeton, N.J.: Princeton University Press, 1989).

15. Warmington, *The Commerce between the Roman Empire and India*, 261–72; Wilfred H. Schoff, trans., *The Periplus of the Erythraean Sea* (New York: Longmans Green and Co., 1912), 167, 28, 39, 49; and H. Rackham, trans., *Pliny's Natural History* (Cambridge, Mass.: Harvard University Press, 1956–62), chapters 20, 32.

16. Rackham, trans., *Pliny's Natural History*, chapter 37, p. 23; Warmington, *The Commerce between the Roman Empire and India*, 200; George Watt, *The Commercial Products of India* (London: n.p., 1908; reprint, New Delhi: Today and Tomorrow's Printer & Publishers, 1966), 891 (page citation refers to 1908 edition); Schoff, *The Periplus*, 73, 192; and *Periplus* 39, 48, 49.

17. *Periplus* 39, 48, 49; James Innes Miller, *The Spice Trade of the Roman Empire, 29 B.C. to A.D. 641* (Oxford: Clarendon Press, 1969), 69, 84, 88; Schoff, *The Periplus*, 168–70; Warmington, *The Commerce between the Roman Empire and India*, 201, 255; Paul Bernard and H. P. Francfort, *Etudes de geographie historique sur la plaine de' Ai-Khanoum* (Afghanistan) (Paris: Centre National de la Recherche Scientifique,

1978), 49.

18. Otto Maenchen-Helfen, "From China to Palmyra," *Art Bulletin*, no. 25 (1943): 358–62.

19. The ethnic background of the Kushans stems from the very complicated migrations of many steppe peoples. Both Western and Asian scholars have written extensively on this topic. The Chinese scholar Taishan Yu ties up loose ends of this issue. See Taishan Yu, *Saizhongshi Yanjin* (A study of the history of the Saizhong people) (Beijing: Press of Social Sciences, 1992), and "On the First Kushan Dynasty," *Journal of Central Asian Studies* (Beijing) 4: 73–96.

20. The dates of the ruler Kanishka are crucial for a better understanding of the chronology of the Kushan Empire. Two international conferences have been held around this issue, but no conclusive agreement has been reached. See A. L. Basham, ed., *Papers on the Date of Kanishka* (Leiden, Netherlands: E. J. Brill, 1968).

21. A great event of Kushan studies was the International Conference on the History, Archaeology, and Culture of Central Asia in the Kushan Period, held in 1968 in Dushanbe, Tajikstan, under UNESCO auspices. In 1974 the conference proceedings were published as *Central Asia in the Kushan Period: Proceedings of the International Conference on the History, Archaeology, and Culture of Central Asia in the Kushan Period, Dushanbe, 1968* (2 vols., Moscow 1974–75) by UNESCO in Moscow, which includes contributions of scholars from many countries.

22. Joseph Hackin, *Recherches archeologiques a Begram, chantier no. 2 (1937)*, DAFA (Mémoires de le Délégation archéologique francais en Afghanistan) t. ix (Paris: Les Editions de'art et d'histoir, 1939).

23. Hackin, *Recherches archeologiques a Begram;* Hackin, *Nouvelles Recherches archeologiques a Begram (ancient Kapici) (1939–40)* (Paris: Imprimerie nationale, presses universitaires, 1954).

2. BUDDHISM AND THE SILK ROAD

1. There was an effort to publish inscriptions of this period in one volume as the second volume of the *Corpus Inscriptionum Indicarum*, but so far only those in Kharoshthi script have been put together as part 1 of this volume. See Sten Konow, *Kharoshthi Inscriptions*, vol. 2, pt. 1 of *Corpus Inscriptionum Indicarum* (Varanasi, India: Indological Book House, 1969). For the inscriptions in Brahmi script dated to this period, see Heinrich Luders, "A List of Brahmi Inscriptions," appendix to *Epigraphia Indica* (Calcutta), vol. 10 (1912); and Luders, *Mathura Inscriptions* (Göttingen, Germany: Vandenhoeck & Ruprecht, 1961).

2. Gandharan Buddhist art has been studied by many art historians. Probably the most systematic research on the topic is Lolita Nehru's *The Origins of the Gandharan Style* (Delhi: Oxford University Press, 1989).

3. John Hubert Marshall, *Taxila* (Cambridge: Cambridge University Press, 1951), vol. 1, p. 238.

4. Marshall, *Taxila*, vol. 2, p. 1–21.

5. Marshall, *Taxila*, vol. 5, p. 74–82.

6. Marshall, *Taxila,* vol. 7, p. 97; vols. 21, 25.

7. *Bodhisattva* was once the appellation for the Buddha before he reached enlightenment. In Mahayana Buddhist texts, however, the term defines a host of characters who were at the threshold of reaching enlightenment but paused to help others cross the ocean of suffering.

8. Xinru Liu, *Ancient India and Ancient China: Trade and Religious Exchanges,* A.D. *1–600* (New Delhi: Oxford University Press, 1988), 96–97.

9. Thomas Burrow, *A Translation of Kharoshthi Documents from Chinese Turkestan* (London: Royal Asiatic Society, 1940), 1.

10. W. B. Henning, "The Date of the Sogdian Letters," *Bulletin of the School of Oriental and African Studies* 12 (1948): 601–15.

11. Yongtong Tang, *Han Wei Liang Jin Nanbeichao Fojiao Shi* (Buddhist history from the Han, the Wei, the two Jin dynasties to the Southern and Northern dynasties) (Changsha, China: Commercial Press, 1927), 512.

12. Yongtong Tang, *Han Wei Liang Jin Nanbeichao Fojiao Shi,* 512.

13. Xuanzhi Yang, *Loyang Qielan Ji* (Memories of holy places in Loyang), ed. Fan Xiangyong (Shanghai: Guji Chubanshe, 1978), chap. 5, p. 266; trans. W.J.F. Jenner (Oxford: Clarendon Press, 1981).

14. Liu, *Ancient India and Ancient China,* 68.

3. Silk Producers outside China

1. Phyllis Ackerman, "Textiles through the Sassanian Period," in Arthur Upan Pope, ed., *A Survey of Persian Art,* vol. 2 (1938; reprint, New York: Maxwell Aley Literary Associates, 1981), 691–92.

2. Xinglang Zhang, *Zhongxi Jiaotong Shiliao Huibian* (History of cultural communications between the west and China) (1930; reprint, Beijing: Zhonghua Shuju, 1977–79), iii, 102.

3. The mutual influences between Western-Central Asia and China on the development of weaving technology and artistic designs have been well studied by Michael Meister, "The Pearl Roundel in Chinese Textile Design," *Ars Orientalis* 8 (1970): 255–67; and Nai Xia, "New Finds of Ancient Silk Fabrics in Sinkiang," *Kaogu Xuebo* (Beijing) 1 (1963): 45–76.

4. H. B. Dewing, trans., *Procopius,* vol. 1 of seven volumes in the Loeb Classical Library series (Cambridge, Mass.: Harvard University Press, 1935), xx, 9–12.

5. *Sanguozhi* (A history of the Three Kingdoms), comp. Chen Shou (233–97 C.E.); commentary by Pei Songzhi (372–451 C.E.) (Beijing: Zhonghua Shuju, 1959), chap. 30, p. 860.

6. You Du (735–812 C.E.), *Tongdian* (A history of institutions), eds. Wenjin Wang and others (Beijing: Zhonghua Shuju, 1988), chap. 193, p. 5,265.

7. Meyer Reinhold did a thorough study on the special role of purple in history, except for that of China, in *The History of Purple as a Status Symbol in Antiquity* (Brussels, Belgium: Latomus, 1970).

8. Adele La Barre Starensier, "An Art Historical Study of the Byzantine Silk Industry," Ph.D. diss., Columbia University, 1982, 76.

9. R. S. Lopez was one of the authorities on the Byzantine silk industry. See Lopez, "Silk Industry in the Byzantine Empire," *Speculum* 20: 1–43. Starensier's 1982 dissertation, "An Art Historical Study of the Byzantine Silk Industry," brought the topic up to date.

4. CONTRIBUTIONS OF RELIGIOUS ACTIVITIES

1. Hui-li and Yanzong, *Daciensi Sanzangfashi Zhuan* (Biography of Xuanzuang), eds. Yutang Sun and Fang Xie (Beijing: Zhonghua Shuju, 1983), 21

2. Japanese scholars made many contributions to Central Asian and South Asian Buddhist studies in recent decades. Seichi Kuwayama, both an archaeologist and a historian, is representative of these contributions. See Kuwayama, *Kapishi Gandara Shi Kenkyu* (History of Kapisa and Gandhara) (Kyoto: Kyoto University, 1990), 280.

3. The cult of saints, especially in the form of relic worship, in medieval Europe was such a puzzling phenomenon in Christian history that many scholars wrote about it. See Peter Brown, *The Cult of Saints: Its Rise and Function in Latin Christianity* (Chicago: University of Chicago Press, 1981). For more on this topic, see Patrick J. Geary, *Furta Sacra: Thefts of Relics in the Central Middle Ages* (Princeton, N.J.: Princeton University Press, 1978).

4. Brown, *The Cult of Saints*, 63.

5. Adele La Barre Starensier, "An Art Historical Study of the Byzantine Silk Industry," Ph.D. diss., Columbia University, 1982, 450.

6. Anna Maria Muthesius's Ph.D. diss. ("Eastern Silks in Western Shrines and Treasuries before 1200," Courtauld Institute of Art, University of London, 1982) on silk textiles preserved in western European churches is the most comprehensive research on the topic. A brief summary of the work has been published as "The Impact of the Mediterranean Silk Trade in Western Europe before 1200 a.d.," in *Textiles in Trade: Proceedings of the Textile Society of America Biennial Symposium* (Washington, D.C.: Textile Society of America, 1990), 129.

7. De Legatione Constantinopolitana, chaps. LIII–LV, in F. A. Wright, trans., *The Works of Liudprand of Cremona* (London: G. Bell & Sons Ltd., 1930).

8. Robert Bertram Serjeant did extensive research to collect literary references on the Islamic textile industry and trade. His collection has been the most important literary source for studying Islamic textiles. It was first published as Ars Islamic, vols. 9–16, from 1942. In 1972 it was published in a single volume, making the reference much easier to use, as *Islamic Textiles* (Beirut, Lebanon: Librarie du Liban).

9. Irene Bierman discussed this interesting phenomenon and analyzed the communication routes that brought Islamic silks to Christian Europe in her Ph.D. diss., "From Politics to Art: The Fatimid Uses of Tiraz Fabrics," University of Chicago, 1980.

5. Nomads and Central Asian Traders

1. You Du (735–812 c.e.), *Tongdian* (A history of Institutions), eds. Wenjin Wang and others (Beijing: Zhonghua Shuju, 1988), chap. 193, p. 5,265.

2. You Du, *Tongdian*, chap. 40, p. 1,103.

3. Samuel N. C. Lieu, *Manichaeism in the Later Roman Empire and Medieval China* (Manchester: Manchester University Press, 1985), 185.

4. B. I. Marshak and Valentina I. Raspopova, "Wall Paintings from a House with a Granary, Panjikent, First Quarter of the Eighth Century A.D.," *Silk Road Art and Archaeology: Journal of the Institute of Silk Road Studies* (Kamakura) (1990): 153, 173.

5. *Jiu Tangshu* (Old history of the Tang dynasty), comp. Liu Xu and others, the Later Jin Dynasty (Beijing: Zhonghua Shuju, 1975), chap. 51, p. 1,346.

6. *Jiu Tangshu*, chap. 195, p. 5,207.

7. Wushu Lin, *Monijiao jiqi Dongjian* (Manichaeism and its spread to China) (Beijing: Zhonghua Shuju, 1987), 90–92.

8. Wushu Lin, *Monijiao jiqi Dongjian*, 94–95.

9. Christopher Beckwith, "The Impact of the Horse and Silk Trade on the Economy of T'ang China and the Uighur Empire," *Journal of the Economic and Social History of the Orient* 34, pt. 2 (June 1991).

10. Nejat Diyarbekirli, "Turkish Contributions of Cultural and Commercial Life along Silk Road," in eds. Umesao Tadao and Sugimura Toh, *Significance of Silk Roads in the History of Human Civilization* (Osaka, Japan: National Museum of Ethnology, 1992), 174.

11. Diyarbekirli, "Turkish Contributions," 175.

12. Guangda Zhang, "Haibo Lai Tianfang, Silu Tong Dashi" (Ships come from Arabia, the Silk Road leads to Arabia), in ed. Yiliang Zhou, *Zhongwai Wenhua Jiaoliu Shi* (History of cultural communications between China and the outside world) (Zhengzhou, China: Henan People's Publisher, 1987), 751; Ibn Khordadhbeh, *Kitab Al-Masalik Wa'l-Mamalik* (Leiden, Netherlands: E. J. Brill, 1889), Chinese trans. by Song Xian *Daoli bangguozhi* (Beijing: Zhonghua Shuju, 1991), 73; S. D. Goitein, *A Mediterranean Society: The Jewish Communities of the Arab World as Portrayed in the Documents of the Cairo Geniza* (Berkeley: University of California Press, 1967), vol. 1, p. 455, note 53.

13. These refer to documents deposited by Jews in the *geniza*, special storage containers for written papers in the medieval period. The papers found in Cairo geniza have been catalogued and studied by Goitein, *A Mediterranean Society*.

14. Goitein, *A Mediterranean Society*, vol. 1, pp. 230, 245.

6. Conclusion

1. An analysis of those movements and interactions can be found in a book by Jerry Bentley, *Old World Encounters: Cross-Cultural Contacts and Exchanges in Pre-Modern Times* (New York: Oxford University Press, 1993).

References

Ackerman, Phyllis. 1981. "Textiles through the Sassanian Period." In vol. 2 of *A Survey of Persian Art*, ed. Arthur Upan Pope. 1938. Reprint, New York: Maxwell Aley Literary Associates, 681–714.

Basham, A. L., ed. 1968. *Papers on the Date of Kanishka*. Leiden, Netherlands: E. J. Brill.

Beckwith, Christopher. 1991. "The Impact of the Horse and Silk Trade on the Economy of T'ang China and the Uighur Empire." *Journal of the Economic and Social History of the Orient* 34, pt. 2 (June 1991).

Bentley, Jerry. 1993. *Old World Encounters: Cross-Cultural Contacts and Exchanges in Pre-Modern Times*. New York: Oxford University Press.

Bernard, Paul, and H. P. Francfort. 1978. *Etudes de geographie historique sur la plaine de'Ai-Khanoum* (Afghanistan). Paris: Centre National de la Recherche Scientifique.

Bierman, Irene. 1980. "From Politics to Art: The Fatimid Uses of Tiraz Fabrics." Ph.D. diss., University of Chicago.

Brown, Peter. 1981. *The Cult of Saints: Its Rise and Function in Latin Christianity*. Chicago: University of Chicago Press.

Burrow, Thomas. 1940. *A Translation of Kharoshthi Documents from Chinese Turkestan*. London: Royal Asiatic Society.

Casson, Lionel, trans. and ed. 1989. *The Periplus Maris Erythraei*. Princeton, N.J.: Princeton University Press.

Diyarbekirli, Nejat. 1992. "Turkish Contributions of Cultural and Commercial Life along the Silk Road." In *Significance of Silk Roads in the History of*

Human Civilization, eds. Umesao Tadao and Sugimura Toh. Osaka: National Museum of Ethnology.

Du, You (735–812 C.E.). 1988. *Tongdian* (A history of institutions), eds. Wenjin Wang and others. Beijing: Zhonghua Shuju.

Geary, Patrick J. 1978. *Furta Sacra: Thefts of Relics in the Central Middle Ages.* Princeton, N.J.: Princeton University Press.

Giles, Lionel. 1957. *Descriptive Catalogue of the Chinese Manuscripts from Tunhuang in the British Museum.* London: Trustees of the British Museum.

Goitein, S. D. 1967–78. *A Mediterranean Society: The Jewish Communities of the Arab World as Portrayed in the Documents of the Cairo Geniza.* 3 vols. Berkeley: University of California Press.

Hackin, Joseph. 1939. *Recherches archeologiques a Begram, chantier no. 2 (1937),* DAFA (Mémoires de le Délégation archéologique francais en Afghanistan) t. ix. Paris: Les Editions de'art et d'histoire.

———. 1954. *Nouvelles Recherches archeologiques a Begram (ancient Kapici). 1939–40.* Paris: Imprimerie nationale, presses universitaires.

Henning, W. B. 1940. *Sogdica.* London: Royal Asiatic Society.

———. 1948. "The Date of the Sogdian Letters." *Bulletin of the School of Oriental and African Studies* 12: 601–15.

Hopkirk, Peter. 1980. *Foreign Devils on the Silk Road.* London: John Murray.

Hui-li and Yanzong. 1983. *Daciensi Sanzangfashi Zhuan* (Biography of Xuanzang), eds. Yutang Sun and Fang Xie. Beijing: Zhonghua Shuju.

Huntingford, G.W.B., trans. and ed. 1980. *The Periplus of the Erythraean Sea.* London: Hakluyt Society.

Ibn Khordadhbeh. 1889. *Kitab Al-Masalik Wa'l-Mamalik.* Leiden, Netherlands: E. J. Brill. Chinese trans. by Song Xian. 1991. *Daoli bangguozhi.* Beijing: Zhonghua Shuju.

Jagchid, Sechin, and Van Jay Symons. 1989. *Peace, War, and Trade along the Great Wall: Nomadic-Chinese Interaction through Two Millennia.* Bloomington: Indiana University Press.

Konow, Sten. 1969. *Kharoshthi Inscriptions.* Vol. 2, pt. 1 of *Corpus Inscriptionum Indicarum.* Varanasi, India: Indological Book House.

Kuwayama, Seichi. 1990. *Kapishi Gandara Shi Kenkyu* (History of Kapisa and Gandhara). Kyoto: Kyoto University.

Lieu, Samuel N. C. 1985. *Manichaeism in the Later Roman Empire and Medieval China.* Manchester: Manchester University Press.

Lin, Wushu. 1987. *Monijiao jiqi Dongjian* (Manichaeism and its spread to China). Beijing: Zhonghua Shuju.

Liu, Xinru. 1988. *Ancient India and Ancient China: Trade and Religious Exchanges, A.D. 1–600.* New Delhi: Oxford University Press.

Liu, Xu, and others, comps. 1975. *Jiu Tangshu* (Old history of the Tang dynasty). Beijing: Zhonghua Shuju.

Lopez, R. S. 1945. "Silk Industry in the Byzantine Empire." *Speculum* 20: 1–43.

Luders, Heinrich. 1912. "Appendix: A List of Brahmi Inscriptions."

Epigraphia Indica (Calcutta) 10.

————. 1961. *Mathura Inscriptions*. Göttingen, Germany: Vandenhoeck & Ruprecht.

Maechen-Helfen, Otto. 1943. "From China to Palmyra." *Art Bulletin*, no. 25: 358–62.

Marshak, B. I., and Valentina I. Raspopova. 1990. "Wall Paintings from a House with a Granary, Panjikent, First Quarter of the Eighth Century A.D." *Silk Road Art and Archaeology: Journal of the Institute of Silk Road Studies* (Kamakura), 123–76.

Marshall, John Hubert. 1951. *Taxila*. 3 vols. Cambridge: Cambridge University Press.

McCrindle, John W. 1979. *Ancient India as Described in Classical Literature*. Westminster: n.p., 1901. Reprint, New Delhi: Oriental Books.

————. 1983. *The Invasion of India by Alexander the Great*. 1896. Reprint, Delhi: Cosmo Publications.

McNeill, William H. 1982. *The Pursuit of Power: Technology, Armed Force, and Society since A.D. 1000*. Chicago: University of Chicago Press.

Meister, Michael. 1970. "The Pearl Roundel in Chinese Textile Design." *Ars Orientalis* 8: 255–67.

Miller, James Innes. 1969. *The Spice Trade of the Roman Empire, 29 B.C. to A.D. 641*. Oxford: Clarendon Press.

Muthesius, Anna Maria. 1982. "Eastern Silks in Western Shrines and Treasuries before 1200." Ph.D. diss., Courtauld Institute of Art, University of London.

————. 1990. "The Impact of the Mediterranean Silk Trade on Western Europe before 1200 A.D." In *Textiles in Trade: Proceedings of the Textile Society of America Biennial Symposium*. Washington D.C.: Textile Society of America.

Nehru, Lolita. 1989. *The Origins of the Gandharan Style*. Delhi: Oxford University Press.

Rackham, H., trans. 1956–62. *Pliny's Natural History*. 10 vols. Loeb Classical Library series. Cambridge, Mass.: Harvard University Press.

Raschke, M. G. 1978. "New Studies in Roman Commerce with the East." In Band II 9.2 of *Aufstieg und Niedergang der Romischer Welt*. Berlin: Walter de Gruyter, 608–1,378.

Ray, Himanshu P. 1994. *The Winds of Change: Buddhism and the Maritime Links of Early South Asia*. Delhi: Oxford University Press.

Reinhold, Meyer. 1970. *The History of Purple as a Status Symbol in Antiquity*. Brussels, Belgium: Latomus.

Sanguozhi (A history of the Three Kingdoms). 1959. Comp. Chen Shou (233–97 C.E.); commentary by Pei Songzhi (372–451 C.E.). Beijing: Zhonghua Shuju.

Schoff, Wilfred H., trans. 1912. *The Periplus of the Erythraean Sea*. New York: Longmans Green and Co.

Serjeant, Robert Bertram. 1972. *Islamic Textiles*. Beirut, Lebanon: Librairie du Liban.

Starensier, Adele La Barre. 1982. "An Art Historical Study of the Byzantine Silk Industry." Ph.D. diss., Columbia University.

Stein, Aurel. 1921. *Serindia*. 5 vols. Oxford: Oxford University Press.

———. 1928. *Inner Most Asia*. Oxford: Clarendon Press.

Tang, Yongtong. 1927. *Han Wei Liang Jin Nanbeichao Fojiao Shi* (Buddhist history from the Han, the Wei, the two Jin dynasties to the Southern and Northern dynasties). Changsha, China: Commercial Press.

Warmington, Eric Herbert. 1974. *The Commerce between the Roman Empire and India.* Cambridge: n.p., 1928. Reprint, London: Curzon Press, Ltd.

Watt, George. 1966. *The Commercial Products of India.* London: n.p., 1908. Reprint, New Delhi: Today and Tomorrow's Printer & Publishers.

Wheeler, R. E. Mortimer. 1954. *Rome beyond the Imperial Frontiers.* London: G. Bell & Sons Ltd.

Wright, F. A., trans. 1930. *The Works of Liudprand of Cremona.* London: George Routledge & Sons Ltd.

Xia, Nai. 1963. "New Finds of Ancient Silk Fabrics in Sinkiang." *Kaogu Xuebao* (Beijing) 1: 45–76.

Yang, Xuanzhi. 1978. *Loyang Qielan Ji* (Memories of holy places in Loyang). Edited by Fan Xiangyong. Shanghai: Guji Chubanshe; trans. by W.J.F. Jenner. Oxford: Clarendon Press, 1981.

Yu, Taishan. 1992. *Saizhongshi Yanjiu* (A study of the history of the Saizhong people). Beijing: Press of Chinese Social Sciences.

———. 1995. "On the First Kushan Dynasty." *Journal of Central Asian Studies* (Beijing) 4: 73–96.

Yu, Yingshi. 1967. *Trade and Expansion in Han China: A Study in the Structure of Sino-Barbarian Relations.* Berkeley: University of California Press.

Zhang, Guangda. 1987. "Haibo Lai Tianfang, Silu Tong Dashi" (Ships come from Arabia, the Silk Road leads to Arabia). In *Zhongwai Wenhua Jiaoliu Shi* (History of cultural communications between China and the outside world), ed. Yiliang Zhou. Zhengzhou: Henan People's Publisher, 743–802.

Zhang, Xinglang. 1977–79. *Zhongxi Jiaotong Shiliao Huibian* (Historical sources of communications between the West and China). 6 vols. 1930. Reprint, Beijing: Zhonghua Shuju.

Zhongmin, Wang, comp. 1957. *Dunhuang Guju Xulu.* Beijing: Zhonghua Shuju.